73 Poems

73 Poems

E. E. CUMMINGS

Edited, with an Afterword, by George James Firmage

Liveright

New York • London

For information about permission to reproduce selections from this book,
write to Permissions, Liveright Publishing Corporation, 500 Fifth Avenue,
New York, NY 10110

Manufacturing by the Courier Companies, Inc.
Production manager: Amanda Morrison

ISBN 0-87140-183-5 (pbk.)

Liveright Publishing Corporation
500 Fifth Avenue, New York, N.Y. 10110
www.wwnorton.com

W. W. Norton & Company Ltd.
Castle House, 75/76 Wells Street, London W1T 3QT

3 4 5 6 7 8 9 0

CONTENTS

73 Poems

|

O the sun comes up-up-up in the opening

sky(the all the
any merry every pretty each

bird sings birds sing
gay-be-gay because today's today)the
romp cries i and the me purrs

you and the gentle
who-horns says-does moo-woo
(the prance with the
three white its stimpstamps)

the grintgrunt wugglewiggle
champychumpchomps yes
the speckled strut begins to scretch and
scratch-scrutch

and scritch(while
the no-she-yes-he fluffies tittle
tattle did-he-does-she)& the

ree ray rye roh
rowster shouts

rawrOO

2

for any ruffian of the sky
your kingbird doesn't give a damn—
his royal warcry is I AM
and he's the soul of chivalry

in terror of whose furious beak
(as sweetly singing creatures know)
cringes the hugest heartless hawk
and veers the vast most crafty crow

your kingbird doesn't give a damn
for murderers of high estate
whose mongrel creed is Might Makes Right
—his royal warcry is I AM

true to his mate his chicks his friends
he loves because he cannot fear
(you see it in the way he stands
and looks and leaps upon the air)

3

seeker of truth

follow no path
all paths lead where

truth is here

4

SONG

but we've the may
(for you are in love
and i am)to sing,
my darling:while
old worlds and young
(big little and all
worlds)merely have
the must to say

and the when to do
is exactly theirs
(dull worlds or keen;
big little and all)
but lose or win
(come heaven,come hell)
precisely ours
is the now to grow

it's love by whom
(my beautiful friend)
the gift to live
is without until:
but pitiful they've
(big little and all)
no power beyond
the trick to seem

their joys turn woes
and right goes wrong
(dim worlds or bright;
big little and all)
whereas(my sweet)
our summer in fall
and in winter our spring
is the yes of yes

love was and shall
be this only truth
(a dream of a deed,
born not to die)
but worlds are made
of hello and goodbye:
glad sorry or both
(big little and all)

5

the first of all my dreams was of
a lover and his only love,
strolling slowly(mind in mind)
through some green mysterious land

until my second dream begins—
the sky is wild with leaves;which dance
and dancing swoop(and swooping whirl
over a frightened boy and girl)

but that mere fury soon became
silence:in huger always whom
two tiny selves sleep(doll by doll)
motionless under magical

foreverfully falling snow.
And then this dreamer wept:and so
she quickly dreamed a dream of spring
—how you and i are blossoming

6

fair ladies tall lovers
riding are through the
(with wonder into colours
all into singing)may

wonder a with deep
(A so wonder pure)
even than the green
the new the earth more

moving(all gay
fair brave tall young
come they)through the may
in fragrance and song

wonderingly come
(brighter than prayers)
riding through a Dream
like fire called flowers

over green the new
earth a day of may
under more a blue
than blue can be sky

always(through fragrance
and singing)come lovers
with slender their ladies
(Each youngest)in sunlight

7

it's

so damn sweet when Anybody—
yes;no

matter who,some

total(preferably
blonde
of course)

or on the other

well
your oldest
pal
for instance(or

;why

even
i
suppose
one
's wife)

—does doesn't unsays says looks smiles

or simply Is
what makes
you feel you
aren't

6 or 6

teen or sixty
000,000
anybodyelses—

but for once

(imag
-ine)

You

8

plant Magic dust

    expect hope doubt
      (wonder mistrust)
        despair
             and right
      where soulless our
      (with all their minds)
    eyes blindly stare

life herSelf stands

9

now is a ship

which captain am
sails out of sleep

steering for dream

10

because it's

Spring
thingS

dare to do people

(& not
the other way

round)because it

's A
pril

Lives lead their own

persons(in
stead

of everybodyelse's)but

what's wholly
marvellous my

Darling

is that you &
i are more than you

& i(be

ca
us

e It's we)

| |

humble one(gifted with

illimitable joy)
bird sings love's every truth

beyond all since and why

asking no favor but

(while down come blundering
proud hugenesses of hate

sometimes called world)to sing

12

Me up at does

out of the floor
quietly Stare

a poisoned mouse

still who alive

is asking What
have i done that

You wouldn't have

13

o
nly this
darkness(in
whom always i
do nothing)deepens
with wind(and hark
begins to

Rain)a

house
like shape
stirs through(not
numerably
or as lovers a
chieve oneness)each
othering

Selves i

sit
(hearing
the rain)un
til against my
(where three dreams live)fore
head is stumbling
someone(named

Morning)

a great

man
is
gone.

Tall as the truth

was who:and
wore his(mountains
understand

how)life

like a(now
with
one sweet sun

in it,now with a

million
flaming billion kinds
of nameless

silence)sky;

15

at just 5 a
m i hear eng
(which cannot sing)
lish sparrows say

then 2 or per
(who can and do
fat pigeons coo)
haps even 4

now man's most vast
(unmind by brain)
more than machine
turns less than beast

at 6 this bell
's whisper asks(of
a world born deaf)
"heaven or hell"

e
cco the uglies
t

s
ub
sub

urba
n skyline on earth between whose d
owdy

hou
se
s

l
ooms an eggyellow smear of wintry sunse
t

17

n
Umb a
stree
t's wintr

y ugli
nes
s C
omprises

6
twirls of do
gsh
it m

uch f
ilt
h
Y slus

h & h
ideou
s 3 m
aybe

o
nce V
o
ices

nobody could
                in superhuman flights
of submoronic fancy
                   be more not

conceivably future than mrs somethingwitz

nay somethingelsestein.   Death should take his hat
off to this dame:he won't be out of work
while she can swarm.   To doubt that in whose form
less form all goodness truth and beauty lurk,
simply to her does not occur(alarm
ing notion for idealists?so what)

all politicians like the sight of vote

and politics,as everyone knows,is
wut ektyouelly metus.   Unbeside
which limps who might less frenziedly have cried

eev mahmah hadn chuzd nogged id entwhys

19

everybody happy?
WE-WE-WE
& to hell with the chappy
who doesn't agree

(if you can't dentham
comma bentham;
or 1 law for the lions &
oxen is science)

Q:how numb can an unworld get?
A:number

20

fearlessandbosomy

this
grand:gal
who

liked men horses roses

& $(in
that
order)is

    wHISpEr

it
left;at the age
of

8

ysomethi
ng
(imagine)

with,pansies

21

why

don't
be
sil
ly

,o no in-

deed;
money
can't do(never
did &

never will)any

damn
thing
:far
from it;you

're wrong,my friend.   But

what does
do,
has always done
;&

will do alw

-ays something
is(guess)yes
you're
right:my enemy

.   Love

22

annie died the other day

never was there such a lay—
whom,among her dollies,dad
first("don't tell your mother")had;
making annie slightly mad
but very wonderful in bed
—saints and satyrs,go your way

youths and maidens:let us pray

23

nite)
thatthis
crou
    ched

moangrowl-&-thin
g stirs(m
id)a
life whats wh

(un)ich(cur
ling)s
    ilentl
y are(mi

dnite also conce
als 2 ph
antoms clutch
ed in

a writewho room)as
hows of
whi
   ne
      climbscr

e
AM
e
xploding aRe(n't

24

insu nli gh t

o
verand
o
vering

A

onc
eup
ona
tim

e ne wsp aper

25

a grin without a
face(a look
without an i)
be care

ful(touch noth
ing)or
it'll disapp
ear bangl

essly(into sweet
the earth)&
nobody
(including our

selves)
will reme
mber
(for 1 frac

tion of
a mo
ment)where
what how

when
who why
which
(or anything)

if seventy were young
and death uncommon
(forgiving not divine,
to err inhuman)
or any thine a mine
—dingdong:dongding—
to say would be to sing

if broken hearts were whole
and cowards heroes
(the popular the wise,
a weed a tearose)
and every minus plus
—fare ill:fare well—
a frown would be a smile

if sorrowful were gay
(today tomorrow,
doubting believing and
to lend to borrow)
or any foe a friend
—cry nay:cry yea—
november would be may

that you and i'd be quite
—come such perfection—
another i and you,
is a deduction
which(be it false or true)
disposes me to shoot
dogooding folk on sight

in heavenly realms of hellas dwelt
two very different sons of zeus:
one,handsome strong and born to dare
—a fighter to his eyelashes—
the other,cunning ugly lame;
but as you'll shortly comprehend
a marvellous artificer

now Ugly was the husband of
(as happens every now and then
upon a merely human plane)
someone completely beautiful;
and Beautiful,who(truth to sing)
could never quite tell right from wrong,
took brother Fearless by the eyes
and did the deed of joy with him

then Cunning forged a web so subtle
air is comparatively crude;
an indestructible occult
supersnare of resistless metal:
and(stealing toward the blissful pair)
skilfully wafted over them-
selves this implacable unthing

next,our illustrious scientist
petitions the celestial host
to scrutinize his handiwork:
they(summoned by that savage yell
from shining realms of regions dark)
laugh long at Beautiful and Brave
—wildly who rage,vainly who strive;
and being finally released
flee one another like the pest

29

the greedy the people
(as if as can yes)
they sell and they buy
and they die for because
though the bell in the steeple
says Why

the chary the wary
(as all as can each)
they don't and they do
and they turn to a which
though the moon in her glory
says Who

the busy the millions
(as you're as can i'm)
they flock and they flee
through a thunder of seem
though the stars in their silence
say Be

the cunning the craven
(as think as can feel)
they when and they how
and they live for until
though the sun in his heaven
says Now

the timid the tender
(as doubt as can trust)
they work and they pray
and they bow to a must
though the earth in her splendor
says May

28

"right here the other night something
odd occurred" charlie confessed
(halting)"a tall strong young
finelooking fellow,dressed

well but not over,stopped
me by 'could you spare three cents please'
—why guesswho nearly leaped
out of muchtheworseforwear shoes

'fair friend' we enlightened this stranger
'some people have all the luck;
since our hero is quite without change,you're
going to get one whole buck'

not a word this stranger replied—
but as one whole buck became his
(believe it or don't)by god
down this stranger went on both knees"

green turns red(the roar
of traffic collapses:through
west ninth slowly cars pour
into sixth avenue)

"then" my voice marvels "what happened"
as everywhere red goes green
—groping blank sky with a blind
stare,he whispers "i ran"

29

the greedy the people
(as if as can yes)
they sell and they buy
and they die for because
though the bell in the steeple
says Why

the chary the wary
(as all as can each)
they don't and they do
and they turn to a which
though the moon in her glory
says Who

the busy the millions
(as you're as can i'm)
they flock and they flee
through a thunder of seem
though the stars in their silence
say Be

the cunning the craven
(as think as can feel)
they when and they how
and they live for until
though the sun in his heaven
says Now

the timid the tender
(as doubt as can trust)
they work and they pray
and they bow to a must
though the earth in her splendor
says May

27

in heavenly realms of hellas dwelt
two very different sons of zeus:
one,handsome strong and born to dare
—a fighter to his eyelashes—
the other,cunning ugly lame;
but as you'll shortly comprehend
a marvellous artificer

now Ugly was the husband of
(as happens every now and then
upon a merely human plane)
someone completely beautiful;
and Beautiful,who(truth to sing)
could never quite tell right from wrong,
took brother Fearless by the eyes
and did the deed of joy with him

then Cunning forged a web so subtle
air is comparatively crude;
an indestructible occult
supersnare of resistless metal:
and(stealing toward the blissful pair)
skilfully wafted over them-
selves this implacable unthing

next,our illustrious scientist
petitions the celestial host
to scrutinize his handiwork:
they(summoned by that savage yell
from shining realms of regions dark)
laugh long at Beautiful and Brave
—wildly who rage,vainly who strive;
and being finally released
flee one another like the pest

thus did immortal jealousy
quell divine generosity,
thus reason vanquished instinct and
matter became the slave of mind;
thus virtue triumphed over vice
and beauty bowed to ugliness
and logic thwarted life:and thus—
but look around you,friends and foes

my tragic tale concludes herewith:
soldier,beware of mrs smith

30

one winter afternoon

(at the magical hour
when is becomes if)

a bespangled clown
standing on eighth street
handed me a flower.

Nobody,it's safe
to say,observed him but

myself;and why?because

without any doubt he was
whatever(first and last)

mostpeople fear most:
a mystery for which i've
no word except alive

—that is,completely alert
and miraculously whole;

with not merely a mind and a heart

but unquestionably a soul—
by no means funereally hilarious

(or otherwise democratic)
but essentially poetic
or ethereally serious:

a fine not a coarse clown
(no mob,but a person)

and while never saying a word

who was anything but dumb;
since the silence of him

self sang like a bird.
Mostpeople have been heard
screaming for international

measures that render hell rational
—i thank heaven somebody's crazy

enough to give me a daisy

31

POEM(or
"the divine right of majorities,
that illegitimate offspring of the
divine right of kings" Homer Lea)

here are five simple facts no sub

human superstate ever knew
(1)we sans love equals mob
love being youamiare(2)

the holy miraculous difference between

firstrate & second implies nonth
inkable enormousness by con
trast with the tiny stumble from second to tenth

rate(3)as it was in the begin

ning it is now and always will be or
the onehundredpercentoriginal sin
cerity equals perspicuity(4)

Only The Game Fish Swims Upstream &(5)
unbeingdead isn't beingalive

32

all which isn't singing is mere talking
and all talking's talking to oneself
(whether that oneself be sought or seeking
master or disciple sheep or wolf)

gush to it as deity or devil
—toss in sobs and reasons threats and smiles
name it cruel fair or blessed evil—
it is you(né i)nobody else

drive dumb mankind dizzy with haranguing
—you are deafened every mother's son—
all is merely talk which isn't singing
and all talking's to oneself alone

but the very song of(as mountains
feel and lovers)singing is silence

33

christ but they're few

all(beyond win
or lose)good true
beautiful things

god how he sings

the robin(who
'll be silent in
a moon or two)

34

"nothing" the unjust man complained
"is just"("or un-" the just rejoined

35

the trick of finding what you didn't lose
(existing's tricky:but to live's a gift)
the teachable imposture of always
arriving at the place you never left

(and i refer to thinking)rests upon
a dismal misconception;namely that
some neither ape nor angel called a man
is measured by his quote eye cue unquote.

Much better than which,every woman who's
(despite the ultramachinations of
some loveless infraworld)a woman knows;
and certain men quite possibly may have

shall we say guessed?"
                              "we shall" quoth gifted she:
and played the hostess to my morethanme

36

if in beginning twilight of winter will stand

(over a snowstopped silent world)one
spirit serenely truly himself;and

alone only as greatness is alone—

one(above nevermoving all nowhere)
goldenly whole,prodigiously alive
most mercifully glorying keen star

whom she-and-he-like ifs of am perceive

(but believe scarcely may)certainly while
mute each inch of their murdered planet grows
more and enormously more less:until
her-and-his nonexistence vanishes

with also earth's
                    —"dying" the ghost of you
whispers "is very pleasant" my ghost to

37

now that,more nearest even than your fate

and mine(or any truth beyond perceive)
quivers this miracle of summer night

her trillion secrets touchably alive

—while and all mysteries which i or you
(blinded by merely things believable)
could only fancy we should never know

are unimaginably ours to feel—

how should some world(we marvel)doubt,for just
sweet terrifying the particular
moment it takes one very falling most
(there:did you see it?)star to disappear,

that hugest whole creation may be less
incalculable than a single kiss

38

silently if,out of not knowable
night's utmost nothing,wanders a little guess
(only which is this world)more my life does
not leap than with the mystery your smile

sings or if(spiralling as luminous
they climb oblivion)voices who are dreams,
less into heaven certainly earth swims
than each my deeper death becomes your kiss

losing through you what seemed myself,i find
selves unimaginably mine;beyond
sorrow's own joys and hoping's very fears

yours is the light by which my spirit's born:
yours is the darkness of my soul's return
—you are my sun,my moon,and all my stars

39

white guardians of the universe of sleep

safely may by imperishable your
glory escorted through infinite countries be
my darling(open the very secret of hope
to her eyes,not any longer blinded with
a world;and let her heart's each whisper wear

all never guessed unknowable most joy)

faithfully blossoming beyond to breathe
suns of the night,bring this beautiful
wanderer home to a dream called time:and give
herself into the mercy of that star,
if out of climbing whom begins to spill
such golden blood as makes his moon alive

sing more will wonderfully birds than are

40

your homecoming will be my homecoming—

my selves go with you,only i remain;
a shadow phantom effigy or seeming

(an almost someone always who's noone)

a noone who,till their and your returning,
spends the forever of his loneliness
dreaming their eyes have opened to your morning

feeling their stars have risen through your skies:

so,in how merciful love's own name,linger
no more than selfless i can quite endure
the absence of that moment when a stranger
takes in his arms my very life who's your

—when all fears hopes beliefs doubts disappear.
Everywhere and joy's perfect wholeness we're

a round face near the top of the stairs
speaks in his kind sweet big voice:
then a slender face(on the mantelpiece
of a bedroom)begins to croon

more particularly at just
midnight this hearty fellow'll exist
—whereas that delicate creature is most
herself while uttering one

a third face,away in the sky
finally faintly(higher than high
in the rain in the wind in the dark)whispers.
And i and my love are alone

42

n
OthI
n

g can

s
urPas
s

the m

y
SteR
y

of

s
tilLnes
s

43

may i be gay

like every lark
who lifts his life

from all the dark

who wings his why

beyond because
and sings an if

of day to yes

44

Now i lay(with everywhere around)
me(the great dim deep sound
of rain;and of always and of nowhere)and

what a gently welcoming darkestness—

now i lay me down(in a most steep
more than music)feeling that sunlight is
(life and day are)only loaned:whereas
night is given(night and death and the rain

are given;and given is how beautifully snow)

now i lay me down to dream of(nothing
i or any somebody or you
can begin to begin to imagine)

something which nobody may keep.
now i lay me down to dream of Spring

45

what time is it?it is by every star
a different time,and each most falsely true;
or so subhuman superminds declare

—nor all their times encompass me and you:

when are we never,but forever now
(hosts of eternity;not guests of seem)
believe me,dear,clocks have enough to do

without confusing timelessness and time.

Time cannot children,poets,lovers tell—
measure imagine,mystery,a kiss
—not though mankind would rather know than feel;

mistrusting utterly that timelessness

whose absence would make your whole life and m͏ʳ
(and infinite our)merely to undie

46

out of midsummer's blazing most not night
as floats a more than day whose sun is moon,
and our(from inexistence moving)sweet
earth puts on immortality again

—her murdered selves exchanging swiftly for
the deathlessness who's beauty:reoccurs
so magically,farthest becomes near
(one silent pasture,all a heartbeat dares;

that mountain,any god)while leaf twig limb
ask every question time can't answer:and
such vivid nothing as green meteors swim
signals all some world's millionary mind

never may partly guess—thus,my love,to
merely what dying must call life are you

47

without the mercy of
your eyes your
voice your
ways(o very most my shining love)

how more than dark i am,
no song(no
thing)no
silence ever told;it has no name—

but should this namelessness
(completely
fleetly)
vanish,at the infinite precise

thrill of your beauty,then
my lost my
dazed my
whereful selves they put on here again

—to livingest one star
as small these
all these
thankful(hark)birds singing wholly are

48

t,h;r:u;s,h;e:s

are
silent
now

.in silverly

notqu
-it-
eness

dre(is)ams

a
the
o

f moon

49

faithfully tinying at twilight voice
of deathless earth's innumerable doom:
againing(yes by microscopic yes)
acceptance of irrevocable time

particular pure truth of patience heard
above the everywhereing fact of fear;
and under any silence of each bird
who dares to not forsake a failing year

—now,before quite your whisper's whisper is
subtracted from my hope's own hope,receive
(undaunted guest of dark most downwardness
and marvellously self diminutive

whose universe a single leaf may be)
the more than thanks of always merest me

50

while a once world slips from
few of sun fingers numb)

with anguished each their me
brains of that this and tree
illimitably try
to seize the doom of sky

(silently all then known
things or dreamed become un-

51

but

he" i
staring

into winter twi

light(whisper)"was
my friend" reme
mbering "&

friendship

is a
miracle"
his always
not imaginably

morethanmostgenerous

spirit.   Feeling
only
(jesus)every(god)

where

(chr
ist)

what absolute nothing

52

who are you,little i

(five or six years old)
peering from some high

window;at the gold

of november sunset

(and feeling:that if day
has to become night

this is a beautiful way)

53

of all things under our
blonder than blondest star

the most mysterious
(eliena,my dear)is this

—how anyone so gay
possibly could die

54

timeless

ly this
(merely and whose
not

numerable leaves are

fall
i
ng)he

StandS

lift
ing against the
shrieking

sky such one

ness as
con
founds

all itcreating winds

55

i
never
guessed any
thing(even a
universe)might be
so not quite believab
ly smallest as perfect this
(almost invisible where of a there of a)here of a
rubythroat's home with its still
ness which really's herself
(and to think that she's
warming three worlds)
who's ama
zingly
Eye

56

"could that" i marvelled "be

you?"
and a chickadee
to all the world,but to me some
(by name
myself)one long ago
who had died

,replied

57

mi(dreamlike)st

makes
big each dim
inuti

ve turns obv

ious t
o s
trange

un

til o
urselve
s are

will be wor

(magi
c
ally)

lds

58

& sun &

sil
e
nce
e

very

w
here
noon
e

is exc

ep
t
on
t

his

b
oul
der
a

drea(chipmunk)ming

59

who is this
dai
   nty
mademoiselle

the o
    f her
luminous
se
  lf
a shy(an

if a
    whis
per a where
a hidi
     ng)est

meta
ph
  or
?la lune

60

2 little whos
(he and she)
under are this
wonderful tree

smiling stand
(all realms of where
and when beyond)
now and here

(far from a grown
-up i&you-
ful world of known)
who and who

(2 little ams
and over them this
aflame with dreams
incredible is)

61

one

t
hi
s

snowflake

(a
  li
   ght
  in
g)

is upon a gra

v
es
t

one

62

now does our world descend
the path to nothingness
(cruel now cancels kind;
friends turn to enemies)
therefore lament,my dream
and don a doer's doom

create is now contrive;
imagined,merely know
(freedom:what makes a slave)
therefore,my life,lie down
and more by most endure
all that you never were

hide,poor dishonoured mind
who thought yourself so wise;
and much could understand
concerning no and yes:
if they've become the same
it's time you unbecame

where climbing was and bright
is darkness and to fall
(now wrong's the only right
since brave are cowards all)
therefore despair,my heart
and die into the dirt

but from this endless end
of briefer each our bliss—
where seeing eyes go blind
(where lips forget to kiss)
where everything's nothing
—arise,my soul;and sing

63

(listen)

this a dog barks and
how crazily houses
eyes people smiles
faces streets
steeples are eagerly

tumbl

ing through wonder
ful sunlight
—look—
selves,stir:writhe
o-p-e-n-i-n-g

are(leaves;flowers)dreams

,come quickly come
run run
with me now
jump shout(laugh
dance cry

sing)for it's Spring

—irrevocably;
and in
earth sky trees
:every
where a miracle arrives

(yes)

you and i may not
hurry it with

a thousand poems
my darling
but nobody will stop it

With All The Policemen In The World

64

"o purple finch
                    please tell me why
this summer world(and you and i
who love so much to live)
                              must die"

"if i
      should tell you anything"
(that eagerly sweet carolling
self answers me)
                    "i could not sing"

65

"though your sorrows not
any tongue may name,
three i'll give you sweet
joys for each of them
But it must be your"
whispers that flower

murmurs eager this
"i will give you five
hopes for any fear,
but it Must be your"
perfectly alive
blossom of a bliss

"seven heavens for
just one dying,i'll
give you" silently
cries the(whom we call
rose a)mystery
"but it must be Your"

D-re-A-mi-N-gl-Y

leaves
(sEe)
locked

in

gOLd
after-
gLOw

are

t
ReMbLiN
g

,;:·:;,

67

enter no(silence is the blood whose flesh
is singing)silence:but unsinging.   In
spectral such hugest how hush,one

dead leaf stirring makes a crash

—far away(as far as alive)lies
april;and i breathe-move-and-seem some
perpetually roaming whylessness—

autumn has gone:will winter never come?

o come,terrible anonymity;enfold
phantom me with the murdering minus of cold
—open this ghost with millionary knives of wind—
scatter his nothing all over what angry skies and

gently
        (very whiteness:absolute peace,
never imaginable mystery)
                         descend

68

what is
a
voyage

?

up
upup:go
ing

downdowndown

com;ing won
der
ful sun

moon stars the all,& a

(big
ger than
big

gest could even

begin to be)dream
of;a thing:of
a creature who's

O

cean
(everywhere
nothing

but light and dark;but

never forever
& when)un
til one strict

here of amazing most

now,with what
thousands of(hundreds
of)millions of

CriesWhichAreWings

69

!hope
faith!
!life
love!

bells cry bells
(the sea of the sky is
ablaze with their
voices)all

shallbe and was
are drowned by
prodigious a
now of magnificent

sound(which
makes
this
whenworld squirm

turns
houses to
people and streets
into faces and cities

to eyes)drift
bells glide
seethe
glow

(undering proudly
humbly overing)
all bright all
things swim climb minds

(down
slowly swoop wholly

up
leaping through merciful

sunlight)to
burst
in
a thunder of oneness

dream!
!joy
truth!
!soul

70

pity his how illimitable plight
who dies to be at any moment born—
some for whom crumbs of colour can create

precision more than angels fear to learn

and even fiends:or,if he paints with sound,
newly one moving cadence may release
the fragrance of a freedom which no mind

contrives(but certainly each spirit is)

and partially imagine whose despair
when every silence will not make a dream
speak;or if to no millionth metaphor
opens the simple agony of time

—small wonder such a monster's fellowmen
miscalled are happy should his now go then

71

how many moments must(amazing each
how many centuries)these more than eyes
restroll and stroll some never deepening beach

locked in foreverish time's tide at poise,

love alone understands:only for whom
i'll keep my tryst until that tide shall turn;
and from all selfsubtracting hugely doom
treasures of reeking innocence are born.

Then,with not credible the anywhere
eclipsing of a spirit's ignorance
by every wisdom knowledge fears to dare,

how the(myself's own self who's)child will dance!

and when he's plucked such mysteries as men
do not conceive—let ocean grow again

72

wild(at our first)beasts uttered human words
—our second coming made stones sing like birds—
but o the starhushed silence which our third's

73

all worlds have halfsight,seeing either with

life's eye(which is if things seem spirits)or
(if spirits in the guise of things appear)
death's:any world must always half perceive.

Only whose vision can create the whole

(being forever born a foolishwise
proudhumble citizen of ecstasies
more steep than climb can time with all his years)

he's free into the beauty of the truth;

and strolls the axis of the universe
—love.   Each believing world denies,whereas
your lover(looking through both life and death)
timelessly celebrates the merciful

wonder no world deny may or believe

AFTERWORD
by
George James Firmage

Four months after Cummings's death in September 1962, his widow, the photographer Marion Morehouse, handed a folder of her husband's unpublished work to the present writer. It contained the typescripts of 29 new poems. Ten of these subsequently appeared in *The New Yorker*; 18 were published for the first time in *73 Poems*; and one ("lively and loathesome moe's respectably dead"), rejected by Mrs. Cummings as a "potential source of trouble," made its first appearance in *E. E. Cummings: Poems 1905–1962* (London: The Marchim Press, 1973), and later in *Etcetera* (New York: Liveright Publishing Corp., 1983).

Fair copies of the poems in the folder, as well as uncollected poems published only in periodicals up to that time, were prepared and arranged by the editor of this edition and returned to Mrs. Cummings in January 1963. After an alternative arrangement by Cummings's first biographer, Charles Norman, had been rejected by Mrs. Cummings, the text was set, proofed, and finally published by Harcourt, Brace and World in October 1963.

The text and setting of the poems in the present edition are based on the editor's copy of the typescript now in the Houghton Library, Harvard University.